Science for the People

Written by **Marilyn Woolley**
Series Consultant: Linda Hoyt

WorldWise™
Content-based Learning

Contents

Introduction

Scientists and scientific ideas

Imagine if you were the first scientist to work out how to save the magnificent bald eagle from extinction out. Or, if you were one of the first scientists to help design a robot that put satellites into space to gather information about the condition of our planet.

Each of the two women in this book – Rachel Carson and Sally Ride – achieved one of these great things because as scientists they asked questions, solved problems, and discovered different ways to protect our planet Earth and its solar system.

More important, these scientists took scientific ideas and made them available to a larger audience through television, radio, books and computers.

Rachel Carson helped save the bald eagle from extinction.

Find out more

The bald eagle has white feathers on its head. Why then is it called a bald eagle?

By widely spreading information about science, these women have inspired a large number of people, and in particular young people, to think about and explore scientific ideas and issues.

Sally Ride was the first female astronaut from the United States to travel into space. She also helped design the robotic arm, which is used to put satellites into space.

How do scientists work?

Scientists set out to solve problems. They try to find out something that no one has known before. They ask questions and think about possible explanations for why something happens.

Then they set up tests and design ways to test their explanations. From the tests, they gather information that either proves or disproves their ideas.

Scientists communicate their ideas in different ways to different groups of people. Sometimes they invite citizens to gather information for them to use in their research. This helps people understand more about science and to take informed action to look after their world.

Find out more

Check recent newspapers. Find an article or a report on a scientific topic.

Asking questions

The process

Results

Scientists ask questions such as:

Why is something happening?

Is the presence of more plastic bags in the ocean causing the numbers of sea turtles to decrease?

How can technology be used to gather new information?

How can we invent a robotic arm that will lift up a communications satellite from a space shuttle and launch it into space?

- Scientists form statements or **hypotheses** about possible answers or solutions, based on what they have already studied or what is already known.
- They set out to test or support these statements.
- They conduct experiments to gather evidence to prove or disprove their hypothesis.
- They present what they have found to other scientists for comment, review and further testing.

The work of scientists:

- ✔ brings about improvements in medical treatments and cures for harmful diseases and illnesses.
- ✔ broadens knowledge about the nature of our planet and other planets.
- ✔ produces and shows the benefits of new technologies or inventions.
- ✔ examines the dangers of existing technologies for humans and other living things.

Chapter 1

Rachel Carson: Environmental scientist

From a young age, Rachel Carson was passionate about the natural environment and writing. At university she studied biology and began her scientific career in the 1930s, working for the Bureau of Fisheries in the United States. In 1943, she was promoted to the position of **biologist** for the US Fish and Wildlife Service. She studied the sea and its animals, and wrote three books that were hugely popular and widely read.

Rachel Carson

While working for the US Fish and Wildlife Service, Carson became interested in the effect of a **pesticide** called **DDT**, which was first used in 1945. It was widely used by farmers to protect their crops from pests and to increase crop production. Carson wanted to know if this chemical caused harm to birds when they ate crops that had been sprayed with DDT.

Did you know?

Rachel Carson was first published at the age of ten in a magazine dedicated to young writers.

The sea trilogy

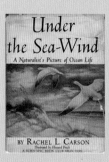

Published in 1941

Published in 1951

Published in 1955

◀ Children playing in a DDT fog left behind by a truck that was spraying DDT to kill insects. When DDT was first used in the 1940s, it was considered safe for humans.

▲ A helicopter spraying a field of crops with DDT.

Carson worked out that DDT got into the food chain and was harming animals other than pests. Because of the buildup of DDT in their bodies, large birds such as bald eagles were unable to absorb **calcium** from their food. The lack of calcium resulted in their eggs having thin shells. Some of these eggs broke easily, killing the baby birds before they hatched.

By the early 1960s, the number of bald eagles in the United States had dropped dramatically to only 487. This species was in danger of becoming extinct.

 Find out more

Find out about one other animal harmed by the buildup of DDT in their body.

Silent Spring

In 1962, Carson published her research findings in the book *Silent Spring*. She chose the title *Silent Spring* because she wanted people to think about a world where there were no birds because of DDT. There would be no birdsong.

These sprays, dusts, and aerosols are now applied almost universally to farms, gardens, forests, and homes – non-selective chemicals that have the power to kill every insect, the "good" and the "bad," to still the song of birds and the leaping of fish in the streams, to coat the leaves with a deadly film, and to linger on in soil – all this though the intended target may be only a few weeds or insects.

Rachel Carson, *Silent Spring*

Many farmers, scientists and chemical companies, however, voiced strong opposition to Carson's book. They wanted to keep using DDT because it protected their crops and increased crop production. They said that Carson's research was inaccurate.

Carson examines a sea specimen for the effects of DDT.

The poison cycle

DDT is sprayed on crop plant.

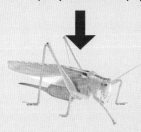

Insects eat the plants sprayed with DDT.

Small animals and birds eat the insects.

Bald eagles and peregrine falcons eat the small animals and birds.

Silent Spring quickly became an international bestseller. The use of DDT and other chemical pesticides became a public issue, and people started a campaign to stop their use. As a result, in 1963, the US government reviewed the use of pesticides on crops.

At the time of Carson's death in 1964, over a million copies of *Silent Spring* had been sold, and her research helped change the law. The US Environmental Protection Agency (EPA) was established and in 1972, it banned the use of DDT in the United States. Groups around the world took similar action and DDT was banned in Australia in 1987.

Unhatched birds' eggs damaged by DDT

Rachel Carson's legacy

Rachel Carson's **legacy** continues today. Her powerful ideas have influenced and changed attitudes to the environment around the world. In 2015, Jo Immig from the National Toxics Network wrote about the legacy of Rachel Carson and *Silent Spring*:

"Her prophetic words about systemic insecticides, designed to turn a whole seed, plant or animal into something indiscriminately poisonous - are especially chilling."

And in 2017, Janine Kitson, Vice Chairperson of the Colong Foundation for Wilderness wrote about *Silent Spring*:

Rachel Carson shared ▲ her love of nature with visitors to her home.

"Rachel Carson's warnings are more relevant than ever."

The Colong Foundation for Wilderness works to protect many of the national parks in New South Wales, such as the Blue Mountains World Heritage Area and Kosciuszko National Park.

Influence of *Silent Spring*

1970s • The number of peregrine falcons around the world declined. This bird became a global symbol for the environmental movement.

1972 • In the United States, the Federal Environmental Pesticide Control Act banned DDT.

1973 • The Endangered Species Act was passed in the United States, to protect animals threatened with extinction, such as the peregrine falcon.

1980s • Carson awarded Presidential Medal of Freedom, the highest civilian award.

1984 • DDT banned in the UK.

1987 • DDT banned in Australia.

2001 • The Stockholm Convention banned the use of DDT in agriculture around the world.

2006 • *Silent Spring* named as one of the 25 greatest books.

Peregrine falcon

Chapter 2

Sally Ride: America's first female astronaut

As a child, Sally Ride loved maths and science. She also loved to play tennis and was a top tennis player. When she graduated from high school, she had to make a tough decision: science or tennis? She chose science and went on to study physics at the University of California in the United States.

As a young science student in 1978, she answered an advertisement in a student newspaper and was chosen from 8,000 applicants to join the National Aeronautics and Space Administration (NASA).

At NASA, Ride worked at the Mission Control Center, where she communicated with the astronauts aboard the shuttles in space. She also helped with the development of a space shuttle's robotic mechanical arm for the second and third space shuttle missions. In space, an astronaut uses this robotic arm to lift a communications satellite out of the shuttle's cargo bay and release it into orbit, or to retrieve it from space and repair it if needed.

In 1983, a significant moment in Sally Ride's life occurred.

DAILY NEWS

18 June 1983

Sally Ride becomes first American woman in space

Sally Ride becomes the first American woman to fly in space on the space shuttle, Challenger on its STS-7 mission.

Ride describes the launch as "exhilarating, terrifying and overwhelming all at the same time." Her job on this flight is the space mission specialist. She will use the robotic arm to release two communications satellites and conduct scientific experiments.

Like all astronauts, she is wearing a flight suit and has to adjust to being weightless in space during her journey. She and other crew members will use high-resolution cameras and radar equipment to take photographs of their work to bring back and share at a press conference.

It is planned that this shuttle will return and land at Edwards Air Force Base, California on 24 June.

The crew of NASA's STS-7 space mission, 4 March 1983. From left to right, (back row) John M. Fabian and Norman E. Thagard; (front row) Sally Ride, Robert L. Crippen, and Frederick H. Hauck.

Sally Ride flew on the Challenger space shuttle again in 1984 to release another satellite, the Earth Radiation Budget Satellite. This satellite was designed to monitor and record any changes in the earth's climate, its atmospheric gases and the **ozone layer**.

On her two missions, Ride travelled about 10 million kilometres and observed Earth as the space shuttle orbited way up in the atmosphere. She could float over to a window and have unique views of the ocean and its coral reefs, volcanoes erupting, dust storms and hurricanes. Ride observed other planets of the solar system and gathered information about the rings around the giant planets, and the volcanoes on the solar system's moons.

Sally wrote up these observations in scientific reports and in books such as *Mission: Planet Earth*.

Sally in the flight deck

A view of the Grand Canyon from space

A view of Earth from space

Sharing her powerful ideas

Sally left NASA in 1987. She set up education programs and started to write books with a science teacher, Tam O'Shaughnessy.

In 1992, they published *Voyager: An Adventure to the Edge of the Solar System* about the two space probes that NASA had launched in 1977 to provide images and information about the planets Jupiter and Saturn. Ride wanted students in classrooms to take part in space missions and she arranged for a digital camera to be put in the crew cabin of five shuttle flights in 1995. Ride called this camera KidSat and explained:

"The astronauts mount that camera so it points to the earth, and we control the camera from the ground. The camera is actually controlled by middle school students from their classrooms via the World Wide Web through a control center at UCSD (University of California, San Diego)."

This idea and technology has evolved into EarthKAM – Earth Knowledge Acquired by Middle school students. This NASA-based educational program enables students and teachers to learn about Earth from the unique perspective of space.

Over 600,000 students and their teachers in 80 countries around the world participate in the program.

Find out more

Are any groups in your school part of EarthKAM? Would you like to participate?

Sally Ride poses with students, 6 October 2010.

Find out more

In 2001, Ride and a team of scientists and educators founded The Sally Ride Science Organization. It aimed to inspire young people in science, mathematics, technology and engineering.

Mission: Planet Earth

Sally Ride also drew on her experiences and work as an astronaut to make young people more aware of climate issues and to warn about the risks of global warming for our planet.

In 2009, Ride and O'Shaughnessy wrote two books for children, calling them to take action to save our planet: *Mission: Planet Earth* and *Mission: Save Our Planet.* In the first of these books, *Mission: Planet Earth*, they explain the complex connections between the earth's water, air and climate systems. If there is a change in one system, it causes changes in the other systems.

Ride used her astronaut's-eye view of Earth to describe to young readers the wonder of looking at Earth from space. During her many space missions, Ride had spent hours looking out the window at Earth, and was inspired by its beauty:

When I looked out the window, I could see winding rivers emptying into blue oceans, mountainsides of a tropical rainforest, and muddy waters of river deltas . . .

She describes the ". . . fuzzy blue line outlining the planet," which is the earth's atmosphere.

It looked so thin and so fragile. . . And I realized that this air is our planet's spacesuit – it's all that separates every bird, fish, and person on Earth from the blackness of space.

"*Science is fun. Science is curiosity. We all have natural curiosity. Science is a process of investigating. It's posing questions and coming up with a method. It's delving in.*"

Sally Ride

Ride goes on to explain how the atmosphere is essential to all life on Earth, and what happens if we change it:

In the last few decades we've started to change that atmosphere. Some of the changes, like the smog hovering over Los Angeles, are even visible to astronauts in space . . . The most dangerous – the one that will affect everything on our planet – is the warming that we now know we humans are causing . . . We all need to think and act differently . . . It's hard to imagine a world without coral reefs, tropical forests, or Arctic ice, but it could happen.

Mission: Planet Earth was followed by *Mission: Save the Planet.* It's a practical book that gives readers lots of ideas on how to make a difference. Both books were popular with students and adults.

 **Did you know?**

Sally Ride and Tam O'Shaughnessy wrote seven science books for children:

To Space and Back (with Sue Okie)

Voyager

The Third Planet

The Mystery of Mars

Exploring Our Solar System

Mission: Planet Earth

Mission: Save the Planet

Sally Ride's legacy

Sally Ride won many awards for her books. After she died at the age of 61 in 2012, Ride was remembered in many ways that recognised her powerful ideas and achievements. A wreath honouring her life was laid at the US Astronaut Hall of Fame.

"Sally was a personal and professional role model to me and thousands of women around the world. Her spirit and determination will continue to be an inspiration for women everywhere."

Lori Garver, former NASA deputy administrator

Musicians wrote songs called "Sally Ride" and "Ride On". Two primary schools in the United States, one in Texas and one in Maryland, are named after her.

Sally Ride on the Challenger space shuttle

In 2013, President Barack Obama honoured Sally Ride's work and achievements by **posthumously** awarding her the Presidential Medal of Freedom.

"Sally's life showed us there are no limits to what we can achieve, and I have no doubt that her legacy will endure for years to come."

President Obama

In 2016, a Sally Ride Science Junior Academy was launched to allow school students from years 6 to 12 to attend workshops and participate in experiments with scientists.

The aim is to help them learn how this research can be applied to many situations in daily life.

"I would like to be remembered as someone who was not afraid to do what she wanted to do, and as someone who took risks along the way in order to achieve her goals."

Sally Ride

Chapter 3 Communicating science

Both Rachel Carson and Sally Ride were determined to improve science communication. Through their writing, television interviews, radio broadcasts and websites, Carson and Ride encouraged people to work with them and other scientists.

Their work has been heralded as mobilising more and more people into citizen science projects. They achieved this by involving adults and school students in learning more about the scientific world and by encouraging them to explore new knowledge, make observations or contribute information or images.

Today, people can easily get involved with citizen science projects, where they can document and upload their observations of the natural environment to help scientists.

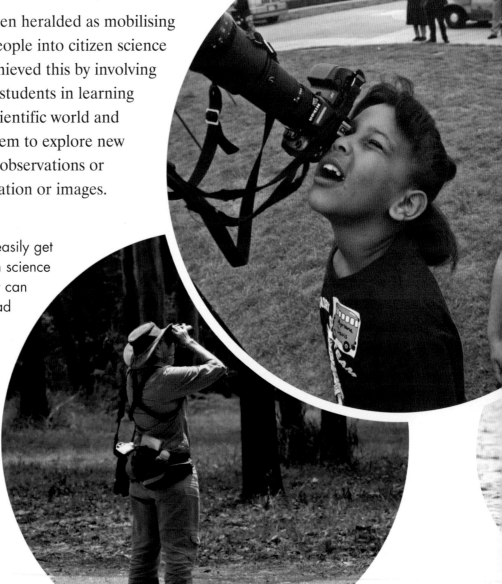

Scientists want your help

With mountains of data to go through, and social media making it easier than ever to reach the public, scientists are asking kids and adults to join in at home. For some projects, you need to gather information about your own house or backyard. Other projects ask people to look at photos of distant galaxies or the bottom of the sea and report back what they find.

Sometimes these pictures are fuzzy or hard to judge – that's why scientists want votes from as many pairs of eyes and ears as they can get. Ready to become a citizen scientist? Start with the projects here and see where they take you. If you cross paths with a wildebeest, don't be alarmed.

Chimp&See

www.chimpandsee.org

Chimp&See needs your help. Their cameras have taken thousands of videos of chimpanzees in many different locations in Africa. They need helpers to watch these videos and make notes to help their researchers learn more about the behaviour of chimpanzees in their natural environment.

In writing your notes, think about things like – What are the animals doing? Are they in a group? What are they eating?

Snapshot Serengeti

www.snapshotserengeti.org

In Tanzania's Serengeti National Park, scientists have set up a grid of camera traps to track how animal species coexist with each other. These cameras snap a picture whenever a warm object moves in front of them. You'll view the photos from these cameras and learn how to classify them.

Sometimes you'll see nothing but grass waving in the sun; other snapshots will reveal a herd of gazelles or a startled baboon.

Bush Blitz

www.bushblitz.org.au

Bush Blitz is Australia's largest species discovery project. You can help by going outside and photographing any new plants and animals you find, such as the common brush-tail possum.

This program began in 2010, and since then 1,553 new animal species, 41 new plant species, 33 lichen species and four new fungi species have been found across Australia.

Play with Your Dog

www.dogsciencegroup.org

It's hard to find a more fun citizen science project than this one. The scientists at the Dog Science Group study dog health and behaviour, and they need your help.

They have lots of dog citizen science projects that you can contribute to, and many involve you observing, training or playing with your dog. You can complete online surveys, upload films or join a research project.

Milky Way Project

www.milkywayproject.org

If you love looking at beautiful pictures of **nebulas**, galaxies and glowing clouds in space, here's a good excuse. Astronomers need your human eyeballs to help them classify these telescope images.

Sometimes it's easier for you to tell the difference between, say, a cloud and an empty space than it is for a computer. Your answers will help astronomers learn about how stars form.

Orangutan Nest Watch

www.zooniverse.org

The Borneo rainforest is being cut down to clear land for farming. This is threatening orangutans on the island of Borneo – one of only two habitats where these animals live.

Orangutan Nest Watch asks you to look for orangutan nests on images taken from drones above the rainforest of Borneo. Understanding the nesting habits of these animals will help protect them.

Stream Watch

www.streamwatch.org.au

Learn more about your local aquatic ecosystem by getting a stream watch kit. This kit will enable you to test the local water quality or conduct a water bug survey twice a year in conjunction with your water quality test.

Because water bugs spend all or part of their life cycles in water, they can indicate environmental changes over time.

Old Weather

www.oldweather.org

These days, we have sophisticated instruments in place all over the globe to capture information about the weather. But to take weather measurements from the past, researchers have to be more creative. One way they're looking at historical climate patterns is by asking volunteers to help transcribe old ships' logs. These books hold detailed handwritten notes about each day's weather conditions, sea ice and noteworthy animal encounters.

What animal is that?

Four times each year, volunteers are asked to go into their backyards and count the birds they see over a period of 20 minutes. They send their observations to Birdlife Australia's website, where scientists analyse the numbers and work out the upward or downward trend.

Other people record the songs of birds in a particular area and send these to scientists. These contributions help scientists monitor responses to habitat or climate changes.

Other volunteers count the numbers of endangered marine species such as turtles or blue whales that they see from light planes or expedition boats.

Some groups use information trackers to record the numbers of **feral** animals or invasive weeds that are causing harm to native animals or plants. This might mean that some of these feral animals are **culled** or moved so that native animal numbers can grow.

Conclusion

In the past, most scientific research that occurred in laboratories or in specialised centres stayed in these places and was available only to scientists and science students. In modern times, new technology has enabled more scientists to communicate to a wider audience.

The passionate women in this book realised that the best way to bring about change in people's understanding of science was to make scientific information available to a large audience. They used radio, television, magazines and books to increase people's knowledge. Other scientists have also changed the way they work. They have designed modern Internet programs that allow people to gather and contribute information on a large range of science topics.

Glossary

biologist a person who studies living things

calcium an element that is found in most plants and animals, and it is important to their health

culled when animals are removed from the herd and killed to reduce or control the size of the population

DDT a chemical insecticide known as dichloro diphenyl trichloroethane that was mixed with oil and sprayed onto crops to control insects

feral returned to a wild state; no longer domesticated or tame

hydrophones devices that are used to listen to underwater sounds

hypotheses ideas or assumptions based on what scientists know, that are yet to be fully investigated or tested

legacy something from the past, such as knowledge, memories or a story, that is relevant and inspiring to present-day people

nebulas huge clouds of gas or dust in space that can be seen in the night sky

ozone layer one of the layers of gases that surrounds Earth and blocks many of the sun's dangerous rays from getting too close to Earth

pesticide a substance such as a spray that is used to kill pests such as insects

posthumously being done after the death of the person

Index